God, Faith & Peace

*Accessing Peace through
Faith in God
Meditations To Live By*

*This book is dedicated to my
grandfather, Eddie Jones,
who always had a peace about
him in addition to endless
words of encouragement for
me.*

God

Each day we can start over
Each second we can start again

There is always an opportunity
to learn therefore there is always
an opportunity to grow

God expects us to follow Jesus
not be Him

Friendship is Gods way of
showing us his love in his
physical absence

God has the ability
To amaze us everyday
We have the ability
To make God smile everyday

Rules are created by people
Choices are created by God

The birth life and death of
Christ are all equally important
Without the birth life and death
there is no birth into Christ life
with Christ or death to self

God expects every effort
Not every right choice

Anything God gives us
Is more than we deserve

God's deepest desire
is to know you
God's only agenda is to spend
eternity with you
That really is it

Sometimes your plan "B"
Is God's plan "A"

Contentment can be found in seeking and being found by God

No detail is too small
No prayer is too big for God

As limited as we are in our thinking it is impossible to fully understand an unlimited God

Satan's purpose is to get you to believe God doesn't love you
God's purpose is to do everything within His power to get you to Heaven because
He loves you so much

Why live to merely exist

You were created in God's image
not He in yours
Therefore you should not place
limitations on Him
What you can do is be inspired
each day as you allow His
image to shine through you

Silence can often be the
resounding gong we need to
hear

Sometimes the best thing you
can do is not do anything

On the roller coaster of life let go
let God and enjoy the ride

With God no one has to
fantasize God can make
dreams into reality

Peace comes from not just
believing in God but from
trusting what He says

Life is a series of bitter
and sweet kisses
Enjoy them all

The word of God gives life as
well as sustains breath

Initially all human life is
spiritually bankrupt until God
makes a deposit

The knowledge of God will be hidden unless you seek it for yourself

God is simple
In our human nature we complicate things

The only thing anyone should ever fear is God and His abandonment
Since He promises to never forsake us fearing Him will keep the latter from happening

God is everything we want to be and be loved by

With God there is always a bigger picture and sometimes You have to focus on Him to see it

God and Satan have equally intense emotions
God is for us and Satan is against us

God might lift you up but He will never let you down

Like the waves of the ocean God never stops moving

All meaningful relationships bring a piece of God into our lives

God is controlled by love
His emotions never lead to sin

The beginning of wisdom is writing that which has been determined wise after application that it might be remembered as well as passed on

God doesn't want us to simply stop by to see Him when we have time
He desires to be our dwelling place while we rest a while

Don't look up, down or around to find God Look within

Faith

My faith cannot be in my faith
Faith can only be in God and it work

There is a road less traveled that is going somewhere

The basic premise of "what if" is worrying about something I have no control over

You can't give your heart without giving yourself

Sometimes the most momentum can be gained from being still

Not every problem requires your solution

A miracle is anything I can't make happen and God does

My life is a painting still being drawn by the Master Artist

Life is like a slide
You slide down and when you get to the bottom
You get up and climb back up to the top

If you close your eyes you may see with your faith

True victory involves continuing to fight long after the game has been won or lost

One person's solution might be another person's problem

Convictions should be the bricks on which emotions are built

You have to have vision to see

It is better to wait on God who has a perfect plan rather than implement a plan that is not His will

There may not be enough time in the day to do everything we want to do

There is however enough time to do everything God needs us to do

If God supplies all our needs we don't need anymore than what we have

Each day brings an opportunity to do something good
look for the opportunity

True love is generally displayed during times of inconvenience

Life is not only what we make of it it is what we practice accept and implement

To stop learning is to stop growing
To stop growing is to start dying

Life is a series of opportunities to pray and have our faith increased

Sometimes God's belief in us has to be enough

The more you understand God not His decisions
The more your faith will be increased

Peace and chaos cannot co-exist

The coolest thing about this race
is to win all you have to do is
finish

Sometimes things are
as they appear
Sometimes they are not
If we seek God neither matters

Don't just take the plank out of
your own eye examine it

If there's nothing you can do to
earn a blessing there isn't
anything you can do to have
one taken away
It's all God's grace

Faith starts with one step
toward hope

Perfection awaits us in the meantime we progress

Logic can stand in the way of faith but people often stand in the way of logic

God requires Faith
Faith leads to Peace

Peace of heart mind and soul means everything

Faith is the beginning of no end

Sometimes a better question than "Why" is asking for help to accept "Why Not"

Life can be like an old puzzle
Some of the pieces can be lost
along the way but that doesn't
negate the picture that we know
exists

Dreams without action become
nothing more than apparitions

There are times when we are
tempted to give up during those
times we should considering
giving in there is a difference

If you find yourself at the end
of your rope tie a knot
hold on for dear life
hang around

When we are on the right path
no matter the odds
The entire universe will often
conspire in our favor
as we attempt to reach God's
destiny for us

Some of the best growth comes
from the worst choices
Stand tall

We are often weakened by our
lack of belief in God's power

While following your dreams
you may be found by reality
and the two become one

The idea of being in control
is an illusion possibly a trap

&
Peace

Since peace can only be given to us by God
we should not allow anyone to take it away

It is hard to be grateful without first being content

Peace knows everything is going to be OK
No matter what

If you don't go after your dreams they may haunt you and perhaps become your worst nightmares

True love can be found by waiting to be found

If writing is a filter for the soul
let the cleansing begin

Peace is a state of being
that comes from
a state of heart and mind

Life is like a balancing scale
You need most things
in equal amounts
Too much of anything can
weigh you down

On the one hand pictures can be
moments in time captured to
remind us of reality
On the other hand pictures can
create an illusion

Life is like a good buffet
there are many choices some of
which you should do without

If the eyes are the window
to the soul
Expression must be
the door to the heart

To pursue perfection is an
endless chase
on a dead end road

To pursue growth is a worthy
step toward a profound
developmental process

Peace comes from being still
and recognizing who God is

Having impure motives is like
continuing to write checks on
an already overdrawn account
The balance will always be
negative

When all else fails
love sustains
When all sustains
You will find love

Loneliness is a nagging
awareness that won't
leave you alone
To know God is to never be alone

In life what is the point
If not to truly live by
Making every effort

Peace and surrender are
directly connected
By surrendering
you gain peace

Time is so precious
No day can be relived
No hour regained
But if we look for
God each moment
Great memories
Can be sustained

A diet of the mind requires the
rejection of unhealthy thoughts
taking in only that which
nurtures the soul

When we live as though we
deserve nothing anything can
be blessing

Sometimes we outgrow more
than our clothes
With spiritual growth you can
out grow people circumstances
and self inflicted wounds

Not all circumstances require
giving up or in
Some simply require giving

Never mistake contentment
for settling there is a difference

Some things
some people
sometimes
You just have to let go

A listening ear
acknowledgement as well as
validation can all be ointment
for the soul

Laughter as well as tears can
always be found among friends

This day will never come again
Enjoy it don't hoard it waste it
or take it for granted
Live without regret

Sometimes life is just plain
and
simple

The fountain of life can often be
accessed through tears of joy
and pain embrace both

May the Peace of God be with you and may your Faith guide you on your journey toward it!

You may reach Q. Avery by email at:

Q.Averysbooks@gmail.com

Copyright © 2011 by Q. Avery
All rights reserved. No portion of this publication may be reproduced or transmitted in any form or by any means, electronic or mechanical, including photocopying, recording or by any information storage and retrieval system, without prior permission in writing by author. No abridgement or changes to the text are authorized.

ISBN Number-9781456539597
Printed in the United States of America 2011

Made in the USA
Middletown, DE
04 August 2015